PICKING UP THE BODIES

NEW AND SELECTED POEMS

JAMES F. CONNOLLY

Fomite
Burlington, VT

ISBN-13: 978-1-937677-81-7
Library of Congress Control Number: 2014948148

Fomite
58 Peru Street
Burlington, VT 05401
www.fomitepress.com

Cover painting: *Calm Before the Storm* — Morgan O'Connell
https://sites.google.com/site/morganoconnellsartwork/

ACKNOWLEDGMENTS

Many of these poems have appeared in journals and magazines, some in slightly different forms, and some with different titles. I would like to thank the editors of the following publications for their generous support:

Angel Face, Antietam Review, Arete, Athelon, Asphodel, Bardsong, The Birmingham Review, Blue Buildings, Borderlands, Texas Poetry Review, Buckle &, Cape Rock, California State Poetry Quarterly, The English Journal, The Evening Street Review, The George Washington Review, The Georgia State University Review, Ghoti, The Kansas Quarterly, The Lake Superior Review, The Larcom Review, The Literary Review, The Lucid Stone, The New Mexico Humanities Review, Oregon Literary Review, Poetry Northwest, The Progressive, Reed Magazine, Rockhurst Review, Sow's Ear Poetry Review, The Taylor Trust, Tendril, The Twelfth Street Review, and *Visions International.*

Many of these poems also appeared in two chapbooks: *Among the Living*, the Jessie Bryce Niles Award, published by *The Comstock Review* and *Last Summer*, the Providence Athenaeum's Philbrick Poetry Award.

* * *

I would like to thank Don Johnson, Paul Laurino, Martin Espada, and Michael Harper for their collegial support and encouragement as these poems were written.

Et introibo ad altare Dei: ad Deum qui laetificat juventutem meam.

CONTENTS

FIRST PICK UP

Daybreak

In ten below cold, December darkness,
you crank the engine, the Volkswagen bug
grr-whirling, grinding, and the clutch popping
to catch the starter – you see yourself back
in the General's jeep,

                      late again that week
to meet the one star general, to deliver him
to his brigade staff. With dawn's light breasting,
the wheel locked, the battery almost dead,
and the clutch ice-held, you began to weep
a young soldier's fear.

                    You can't move the gears,
gloves too thin, hands numb, and you're late again
to teach the lesson on the urn. Mr. Keats
means nothing today:

                    the General returns
your snappy salute and shouts "the bumper":
the C.G.'s one star and flag are missing: "sorry,"
a child's foolish plea, won't cut your fuck-up
and another day of mistakes is on.
"A marvelous day for war," he says.
He smiles. "Get your head out of your ass."
You're a private caught in a jacklight.
You're dumb and fatigued. Your head is where?
You won't remember the body bags.
You're stuck in the bug. You need a jump-start.
What neighbor to call? That one star's bumper.
His son killed himself with the pearl-handled
pistol, his father's .45, the prize
the general called his "Patton." Why this
today? Yesterday you were in Browning,
reaching for more than a man can handle.
You'd like to call her, your brothers, your life –
and what's an insult? What you can't get back.
You're sixty-four and ought to quit.

In twenty years, you're sure to be dead-tagged.
You're waiting. You want the cold bug to start.
You want that hard-nosed one star at close range –
to say what? You'd give anything to bring
her back, happy and among the living.
What's a heaven for? You don't understand
how an engine works. If you could, cold-eyed,
you'd coldcock terror with another chance
and lift the cadavers from their coffins.
The cables you never replaced are shot.
You ought to buy a new car, go to
Florida to forget the dead, to let
the poems disappear, to abandon
the lessons, the lectures, all the ideas
that can't bring her back. At the cemetery,
at your mother's grave, the Chrysler broke down.
And isn't it sad for an aging man,
after all these years, to still mourn
his mother's suicide? To still believe
he could have saved her? This is what life is
you say to yourself. You've got one try left,
and you twist the key to start the machine.
It catches. It moans its way to *rroom*,
and you're backing up, turning carefully,
pumping gas, hoping the line's not frozen:
you're driving to class, to the little town,
mountain-built with a peaceful citadel,
emptied of its folk, today, a pious morn.

Growing Up in a Funeral Home

In the freight yard behind
the funeral home where you lived
through a thousand deaths,
cars uncoupled and rumbled down
steel rails that gleamed in the moonlight.
They groaned like beasts
in a prehistoric cortege.
Their hearts pulsed out steam, cinders and ash.

On some nights the magenta
light crept under the door
of the room of caskets and wakes.
It rose in a mysterious miasma
and entered your sleep
with its diagrams of death:
old O'Brien's bald head,
the skinny kid's bullet hole
that gave way to maggots too soon,
the woman's crimson breast
charred with black lines –
that cold blue penis, limp
and still soft in stiffening flesh.

Each face was a kind of teacher,
each body a silent lesson.
But you swore you never saw it,
you never heard the grieving voices,
the vaults clamping shut.
Your ears rushed in the sound
of freight trains clanking down the line,
in the loud breathing of your heart
chugging in and chugging out –
out of your body and into the night.

Ten Years Old

and we joined the altar boys,
my brother and I, happy souls
that sang church Latin for our priest,
Father Cormier, so handsome,

so dashing – and kind as a nun.
We loved him. Our Father. For two years
we cleaned his sacristy, waited
on him like two little butlers

attending to the orders of the day.
And then, before Easter, we caught
her with him, Joe Brady's mother,
in her car, lurching, hands and breasts,

behind the rectory, twilight,
early April's hold on winter,
every *mea culpa* lined up
like clothespins on the rope,

the pulley squeaking,
the laundry reeled in, the dusk light
hauled suddenly away and we
couldn't, wouldn't, didn't say a word.

An Orphan's Novena, 1956

The candles draw him to prayer, to light,
for the reposal of the departed,
perpetual life, and wick after wick,
he ignites the church in little fires,
his face lit in the flickering of flames.

He rises to lay out the pastor's vestments,
to put on cassock and surplice, to pray
for nine days, for nine nights, indulgences
that he will tally in a small, black book
to save their lost souls, those who gave him up,

their stories of sin, and their dead flesh dead—
to chant the ejaculations of faith
in line after line from the studied text—
nothing forgotten and all forgiven,
each word by rote and all for nothing.

Jesus

When I was sixteen, I had faith
in pain. After practice or a game,
I limped into the training room
where the coach cut the tape on my ankles
and ripped it from my skin. My calves
were as smooth as a girl's.
He sent me to the whirlpool
where I bathed until everyone left.
I showered, dressed, and walked to my car,
slowly, feeling sore spots, breathing
the cold of the autumn night.
When I broke my thumb in a game I lost,
I drove home from the hospital on a night
without a date, the sky starless, the thought
of becoming a priest slipping away
like a ball brushing the tips of your fingers.
The best was the day I broke my nose
against Mission High, a 6-0 loss
in November sleet, the muddy field freezing up
before the game's end. I hurt all over.
I sat in the ER for two hours, waiting
to be taken. No one was there.
Eventually a doctor appeared, patched me up,
and told me to go home. I drove
past Bayview Package and the shipyard
to a house where my parents slept in their rooms
and the coffee burned in the dark.
I didn't turn the lights on.
I didn't call the girl I'd been dreaming of for weeks.
My head ached. I didn't take the pills
and I wouldn't take a drink.
I went out to the back porch
and sat in the cold for an hour and a half,
the greatest night of my life.

First Pick Up

The rain is on the hood again
and the stomach turns concertina wire.
It is the headlights, the blurred voice
of "Follow me, son, it will be easy."

Boris Karloff will always loom
as part of it. At fifteen, a thrill mattered,
but it is the Narragansett bottle
that keeps the hold on now.

The second time was an old man
on the third floor of a Salvation Army house.
He had hollow cheeks and gizzardy neck.
His body wriggled like a half gone catfish.

I didn't mind cleaning the mess on the sheet
while my father's thick hands grabbed the trochar,
but the fish smell made me think again.
"Put the gloves in the basket, son."

Crowley and Loftsky were the first
and that night he had advice on the dead studs:
"They went too fast. Hell raisers.
Remember son, moderation."

Loftsky looked like he was sleeping,
but Crowley held it between his legs,
and the edges of the rooted bottle oozed forward
up through the stomach and into the mind.

Finding the Undertaker, My Father, Drunk, Sitting in the Kitchen, the Shades Pulled Down in the Middle of the Afternoon

I could say it's 1958,
the world beginning to comprehend the physics
of explosion, the frictions of change.
Or that it's whiskey
when I open the door, April's sunlight
a gold magnet pulling you from your chair,
blinding your small, dark eyes.
Or that you are a man who has lost
an infant, a child, a mistress,
a wife – she's crying, you say,
praying her rosary.
You tell me how you've learned cancer
can give a body a long run of courage,
something to rail against,
something to whisper to the world.
Listen, you say, we are white bones
taking root in black earth,
things that break like chalk.

Or I could say
that Ike's on the radio
and Oppenheimer's losing his grip –
or that you and I have stopped
to look out the door
to see the finches hiding
in the bell-shaped flowers
of the forsythia, that you put your arm
on my shoulder and entered the living –
or that the coroner didn't call that afternoon,
the bodies of boys, nine-year-old twins,
stabbed a hundred and stabbed eighteen
and stabbed a hundred and eighteen times.

You had to embalm them, testify
on the technicalities of wounds,

the angles, the depth, your professional opinion
to confirm the actual time –
to put the madman away,
the man I came to know as "Olsen."

The point is
we were there that day and you told me
all about bones and teeth and madmen.
You poured me whiskey to explain, once again,
how you went to war and came back alive,
how you blew that Jap's head off,
how a .45, placed at the base of the skull,
works, so easy, you said, and so quick,
like the closing of an eye.

The Dead Bury the Dead

We did. My grandfather, the funeral director,
left the embalming to my father and me, surgeons
who cut and stitched but never saved.
Adorned in golf shirt, poplin gray trousers,
penny loafers and a tartan tam-o'-shanter,
he led me into his back yard that October afternoon
to pick apples from his trees.
We never talked about death, the fish-eaten
body on my father's prep table,
the mutilated twins the madman cut up
in February, Tinsley's suicide by rope
in May, the stillborns, the nine-year-old girl
I picked up in late August, her spinal meningitis
and the shots I took to keep the bacteria out of my body –
the sun in my eyes, following his direction,
I dutifully plucked the fruit. He told me
John Mcintosh, a Canadian, found the apple
that bears his name, that apples originated
in Afghanistan, that Johnny Appleseed's real name
was Jonathan Chapman – we never acknowledged
grandfather's penis dangling out of his drunken fly:
the secretary, Mrs. Jewell, women
on the street who cried out –
how the Chief of Police looked
the other way when my grandmother
took the undertaker and locked him up
to come back shocked and sober,
another man each time, the look
in the eye gone, his cadence a beat
different, the words slower –
I picked the apples. He placed the good ones
in bushel baskets, tossed the bruised
and scabbed over the stone wall.

Beating the coming dusk,
we piled our harvest in the garage
and he poured the between-you-and-me
whiskey into coffee cups.

I was seventeen.
My mother and father were drinking
through a party that would kill them
before they reached fifty-one.
My brother was beating a weaker
boy into a bloody mess.
My sister was becoming a man,
preparing to cry all her life.
This all happened. You can't make it up.
We picked the big apples
and threw the little ones away.
We kept lies in a grand espionage:
Winesap, King, Russet, Mcintosh, Northern Spy – I loaded
the hearse with apples and cases of rye,
ordered to take the goods to the monsignors
who would sit before the grieving families
and tell them where to bring the bodies:
I drove into the nightfall, through the city,
from rectory to rectory, delivering the secret
deal, taking in the leaves that swirled
through the beams of the headlights,
smelling all the apples and sober enough,
just enough, to hold the wheel.

The Director

I arranged everything,
carried myself like an actor
to light candles and place flowers,
raised my arm and the hearse
rolled – my face, dead pan.
But after each day's shooting,
I held dead men in the arms
of my dreams. Sleep became a burden.
I lay with flesh touching my lips,
purple shadows waking my room in the whine
of the dead, my children
calling from buried
faces: cross-eyed and slack-jawed,
the stiff ashen skin of trowelled-out
bodies tossed into the night
by the gods of the dead
who make the living into life-sized
dolls, B-filmed horrors, folding
and collapsing, conjuring up
the rerun dream of deviled
blood that sears the skin,
that boils, rises from sleep
and

once

a corpse sat up on me,
sneered like the jackdaws
in my dreams of the burned
woman, who looked like
my wife, the meningitis
girl reincarnated
in my child's flesh, and Keach,
my old dead friend,
Walter, whose cavity I tapped,
whose body I made up
ten years younger.
I lied and prayed

in the silence before the dream,
died a thousand times
and drew lines on the decomposed
flesh.
I mean

I sold caskets
where the bodies lie
for living.
For a living I tried

to love

the work, the grief, the dressing
up each day to bury
every dream. The undertaker,
the embalmer, the funeral

director –

a job

of skin and bone and knife –
panning, tracking, zooming in
on the closest of angles –
the dead all reeled and canned
away – I mean

it's the way

I made my life.

The Undertaker's Wife

I want to remember the dead,
the fish-eaten eyes, buttonholes
in blue-white dermis—and that girl,
meningitis, her tiny breasts--

a man who cut and never stitched,
who touched skin like braille, smelled the smell
of blood, formaldehyde,
the throat in its last breath.

You can live with death just so long.
Scotch and rye, we drank into night,
stillborns who died in the wrong line of work.
The bodies killed us. And our sons

died into corpses, cadavers and bones,
our home a funeral, caskets and cash
that would never end. And oh Jesus,
all of that grief, that long, dead prayer of flesh.

The Undertakers: My Mother, My Father

Dying
Is an art, like everything else.
I do it exceptionally well.

"Lady Lazarus," Sylvia Plath

1.

Mother, there were late afternoons
of early snow dusting the ground
like down, and without sound
you drift in from the cold,
a long dark coat, your mind
on fire, your hands frozen.

And then, waiting, always waiting
for that embalmer man
to come out of the dark in his
homburg and black topcoat,
plodding in like a flabby old admiral
with the day's death stories,

you sit by the window,
a made-up ghost
trying to disappear into childhood.
He sloshes his way through this week's stories:
a Marine, home on leave, washing windows,
fell twenty flights to a splattering end;

a drunken old woman went up in flames
in her nightgown; the O'Brien's stillborn;
some man changing a flat was whacked
into his trunk by a trailer truck,
imprisoned in fire, and had to be
peeled out of molten enamel.

2.

In the dusk light that sends
men to their death, he dies alone,
snapping from sleep to rigid pose:
eyes open, fingers spread out
like a possessed preacher.

The Y.M.C.A. clerk tells her
"he drinked himself to death."
Like light churning up dust,
she collects old war pictures,
Navy medals of Pacific valor,
his watch and college ring,
his clothes and unmailed love letters

and brings them home. "He died
in glory on a carrier,"
she says, "the rest was an encore."
She slits her wrists like a surgeon
and leaves sharp instructions:
"solid mahogany – a one day wake."

And when the grass had covered,
I searched through their papers,
found a letter from his commander
who wanted aircraft stories
for a new book: "Please send names of children
and wife, your occupation, wife's occupation."

Death I told him. Death. Just death.

My Sister How I Taught
a Lesson on Child Abuse

Details.
Two days ago we made posters
for the Massachusetts State Commission
For the Prevention of Cruelty to Children
and yesterday I gave a lesson
on how to write about it.
Details I told them. Details.

We made lists, wrote poems,
talked at the bruise of it,
and I felt like an estranged
lover who makes jokes to say
it doesn't matter – it's really
not real. I told stories.
I lied. And what I left out
was the sound of our father's
drunk craze in your ear,
how a secret in our house
was more than love's aberration.
I tried to laugh. I kept
the students light, everything
just right: light, light,
nothing large and heavy
like his body collapsing on yours
in failure he could never
understand. And it was all
all right until I thought of you
locked away again, one more
December, the Christmas rush
rushing all over you until
the world's light snapped –
a crack and it was off,
the nightmare on,
love never right
and every touch as wrong as wrong.

The details got lost
and I told the truth. I saw
the night snow falling outside
hospital windows, you staring
at its drift through holiday lights.
I told them how I saw you,
sister, baby sister, pretty
little sister, still in the arms
of a dead father, how you are watching
busy shoppers goose-stepping into crowded stores
and the whole city marching to the beat of time.

Ablution

That Saturday,
stripped down
to his boxer shorts,
in front of the ice-box,
drunk into his mind,
Billy Harris's father said,
"The skirts cut off your cock
'n balls and shove 'em
down your throat."
His sad eyes chased us out
into the July sunlight
that warmed all over us.
"My father," Billy said,
"got trouble."

In the dusk of that afternoon,
we skipped flat stones out
and on and over the surface
of Carter's Pond.
Our arms grew weary.
The smooth gliders skimmed
into hordes of gnats
and mosquitoes that whined
over and around us.
That was the year Billy's mother
went out to hang herself,
casually, miserably,
the September rain falling
for days and nights,
a county record,
the harvest rich,
and the fields, the lawns
a thick lush of green.

God Watching

At sixteen, on Saturday afternoons,
we went to confession at St. Casmir's.
The priest blessed us in Polish
and never understood our sins:

> *Father; all through geometry class*
> *I watched Mary Bromley's breasts*
> *rise and fall – I believed I was*
> *breathing with her: I masturbated*
> *and will never do it again. I broke*
> *a halfback's nose with a forearm.*

After getting clean, we went to the cemetery
and drank into dusk. We believed in football,
that downfield blocking could take us
to the Queen of Victory
and the love of cheerleaders.
We believed we'd never live
beyond twenty-one.

At forty-two, watching my children
dive from a small cliff into the sea,
I'm scared as hell of hell.
In one way or another, God,
the nuns still have us – the one
with the Ph.D., the lawyer, me,
and the one who stepped on the mine,
too young to feel the fear. We learned
the grammar of how nothing in the world
could frighten us. Your hand is in us
and we stumble on, believing that the hearse
that takes us to the grave
takes us home. Watch over us, God.
We need forgiving and we still try to pray.
We're working hard every day,
taking our lives in the mystery of accidents.

LAST SUMMER

Memory

It's what we can't see
that gets us.
                        You recall
your mother crying
into pieces of jewelry
she holds in her hands,
telling you to stay inside,
that you can't go out and play –
and you're begging her to go
to where your mind forgets,
a place behind that left hook,
that blindside block –
those boyhood places
that still ache when December mornings
enter your bones –
                        that day she took a life,
her own, you say, seeing nothing: thirty-two
years and all you have is her bruised skin,
a dark blue, a dead body
and, now, a knee that locks up,
teeth that won't line up,
a jaw that never closes right.

Last Summer

When the Tilley's tomcat climbed our oak tree
at the backyard party, and took the baby jay,
whole, in one bite, we were taken. Two days later
the jay's mother signed the sky with screeches,
calling in a god-awful sound – and then,
raiding the cat, flying down in attacks
that kept us all spellbound, it clawed
at the cat's back, swooped and fell,
rising in that sound, descending in vengeance.
It went on for days. The cat cowered
until the fitful jay zeroed in, once again, to kill –
and then it was dead, plucked from flight,
the cat's teeth biting,
its paws ripping.

And then that long June our daughter survived:
off the coast of Nantucket, she went down
with two boys, the freshly painted bottom
of the *Amberjack* gleaming in the sun.
They did their best to wait, holding
the boat for the rescue that would have to come.
At dusk, they swam toward land,
clutching a cushion, a triumvirate scissoring
toward a thin line that vanished in the dark.
They kicked. They paddled. They cried
into a splashing of water, gulping,
stroking in panic to stay warm.
She said kick, kick, and they prayed to God
until the cold, cold fluttering of death
took the boys away, down deep, her free hand
letting them go to the stone world
of fish, she alone left to see
the helicopter whirring in the dawn.
And in her living we had to hold on
to newspapers that defined the horror –
the tragic drowning of a choice made wrong –
a waking she will not escape
since she was left among the living.

She stalks our house, moving
from room to room in a place we call land.
She will not answer mail. She cries. She cleans
her body on the hour, scrubs her skin
and orders the possessions of her desk.
She washes the floors, the front steps, the door,
all the sinks, the toilets, baskets of clothes.
Her tan has faded. She grows thin, thinner.
She is all water, and when evening comes,
she walks the beach and calls for them.
Sometimes, she wears Bobby's baseball cap,
Tim's jacket – she's out there tonight, roaming
under the harvest moon, chanting to a neap tide
that ripples the sea, throwing rocks until her arm aches,
calling their names, calling boy, boy ....

Guarding Monet

for Michael S. Harper

He posts at the exhibit's opening,
a slouching sentry who watches white skin
move from frame to frame, the paint impressing
the room: restless skeins of linear
brush strokes, the light falling on the surface

of ponds that reflect, in the distance,
the vertical trees and sky, lily pads,
their receding horizontal islands
beyond his belief: to himself, he says,
if you've seen one water lily, you've seen

them all. In his black suit and black necktie,
the knot tied too large, his thick neck bulging
from a white shirt that is one size too small,
his shaved skull gleaming under the bright lights,
he looks like a young Hagler at the edge

of the ring, waiting for the bell, waiting
for Japan, Paris, Venice, Giverny –
the tall pale woman who stops to ask him
about *The Japanese Bridge*, eloquent
sounds that flood his ears, the bridge that dissolves

into a blue-green silhouette against
a painted cloud of citrus hues, the bridge
covered by a pergola enveloped
with leaves of wisteria and, waiting,
he nods no and points her toward the tour guide.

He could be anywhere, standing, waiting
to make his mark on the colorful world
of dots and dashes, feints and jabs, quick hits
of money and fame, but he is right here,
waiting for the thief who will never come.

My Father's Mother: Peter Bent Brigham Hospital, 1963

Her nightgown caught it, the stove's gas flame—
and then the gold blaze, her body lit up,
her flesh a charred dress of black and red.

He wept in silence. I drove him to her.
He drank his whiskey, a man on fire,
his private burning, the rain on the hood

that shilly-shallied in the wind. He cursed.
He called out her name. He said he believed
in her coming back to skin, a return

to water beading on her arms, her legs,
her breasts, her face—he loved her life too much—
and I took wrong turns, got lost on the streets.

The doctors wouldn't let me in her tent.
She died in two months. We drove in bad words,
the trip each week a pointed pain that held

our anger, and I wanted to see her,
the room forbidden, to see the creature,
the woman burned beyond recognition.

Night Tour, Kilmainham Jail, March, 2000

for Carl and Glenn

Father O'Brien had hard answers
for all our sins. We practiced Latin
under his quick eye and confessed our dreams.
Behind the rectory, we hid and waited
to catch him with her, the dark-haired mother
of our friend, an oath we swore in secret.

Four decades later, I stand in this jail
under a moon as perfect as a host,
recall O'Brien's stories of Home Rule,
remember that parked car, lurching, his hands
in her hair, her blouse, their singular moan,
how three acolytes watched the truth of flesh.

In a war I saw only second hand
you became names on the Washington wall
I've never touched. Here, the jail guide points out
plaques and names, and the tourists try to find
their past in third generation glory.
I stand at the cross where Connolly died.

Dragged from his hospital bed, he became
a crucifixion spectacle, twelve wounds
in his chest, James Connolly, patron saint
of the rebellion – and I can't own it,
the myths and terrible beauties living
in lines that record how the young die brave.

With its bullet hole stars, this sky turns me
back to you. When O'Brien left
in clandestine transfer, we sipped church wine
in the sacristy and filled the bottles
with water to protect our Irish theft.
On the vestibule door we knifed our names.
Tonight's moon and stars shed light
all over this scene of jail house slaughter,

the names on the walls shining the stories
of brother betraying brother, unholy
ghosts stalking the cells, young men calling out,
their wounds dripping real, honest to God, blood.

Nightmare

The night the Firestone factory burned to the ground,
your husband woke me, told me to get dressed,
and the embalmer and his apprentice son
went to claim the dead.
It's hard to remember: the fire engine,
the riverbed lost in steam, elms smoldering,
voices booming at the discovery of two more men.

At seventeen, it was work:
the bodies filled our house, a home of rosaries,
the grieving in their weeping.
And you, silent mother, you walked across the parking lot
each morning like a ghost in search of her body.
And now I want to tell you that factory wakes me
in the hour before light:
I see a man's charred chest, his face a look
Lon Chaney would have envied.

A young woman reappears in the rubble, a face I've seen before.
She has no eyes, no ears, no nose.
She says *mercy.* She says *miracle.*
Through the smoke, daybreak becomes
a coffin of bronze, lilies in a false dawn
that will not disappear. I'm in the hearse,
and I see you, again, holding that woman,
my hands searching, fumbling
for a roll of clean white tape.

Memoirs of a Fireman's Daughter

The back door opens.
You drop your coat,
shed the slick rubber
of your night,
talk the flames quiet.
In my sleep
I remember soot.

Then, behind the door,
voices of thieves,
beggar language,
stealing the rustle of the house:
everything is blind.

Your pressed lips,
the soft mouth,
giant, silent muscles,
the black communion
of coffee
and your morning body:
You tell dark stories
of flesh and wood.

Stories I cannot hear,
should not hear,
will never remember.
There are words now:
charnel, charred, charcoal...
mother becomes a ghost.
I play your charwoman,
become the charlatan.

I remember snow,
oil on your hands,
the bandana voices
planning my life
in smoke, in babies...

the bandit voices
sound soft
as ashes...
I remember
your fire.

Lockdown

for my sister

We have the drill, again, today,
the words of Columbine, Virginia Tech,
and Batman's dark night admonishing us
to be vigilant. In your eighth grade year,
chastised by the priest and thrown out
of catechism, you and your best friend
blew up his Chrysler: oily rags,
newspapers, and a match. No one found out.
You confessed to me, our secret forever.

Until now. I've kept it locked inside me.
You've kept my secrets too. Do you remember
the gold helmet that you snapped tight
for our games, the backyard touchdowns
you racked up on the long, green lawn
behind our old house? I see you again,
there, running, laughing, and so happy
that no one can catch you. I secure my classroom door,
certain that I'm the one who caught you, lost you,
and fumbled your dreams, the one who could not,
and would not, keep us safe.

Christmas Lights

for my brother

Our father drives out of Boston through streets of Chestnut Hill
into the gloaming gray of back roads salted down by plow trucks.
He drinks a beer and watches snow fall through his high beams.
Cases of whiskey and poinsettias fill the back of the hearse

that held, the night before, Mrs. Hicks, who hanged herself
from a pipe in a split-ranch basement. You asked why
and he said *Nuts...get in the car*. And we drove
to the funeral home to help him embalm another body.

Christmas Eve, thirty years later, divorced in Albuquerque,
you call to say you've hung white lights in your apartment,
that you're learning to be a better man and just need
more time. You ask me to remember Ireland and that winter

we entered the trade, his apprentices in the business
of death, how the ground, frozen, kept graves waiting,
how our mother lived on bottles of Valium. Grace, you say,
got us through that year and will again. There's hope

in a new year, you laugh, in this night's full moon.
At home, here, the week promises a Canadian cold front
moving in, and I listen to our pauses until we stop
on the same word as if we've come to the end of a prayer.

DESIRE

The Staging of Charles "Sonny" Liston

"Clay...is the first Negro athlete I have ever known,
the man who will mean more to his people
than Jackie Robinson was, because Robinson is
the white man's hero. But Cassius is the Black man's
...because the white press wanted him to
lose because he is a Muslim." -- Malcolm X

You can tell us the truth, Sonny.
Nobody is going to call you "the monkey"
and we've got nothing at stake.
You've played the dumb brute long enough,
the foil to Elijah and Allah
in a long contest that's on
the other side of memory.

We're standing here for the truth,
waiting for the "Brown Bomber"
to rise up and say
"Sonny was the smart one" –
not the jumpy kid whose willowy left jabs
got smarter as the rounds took away your shoulders
and your arms. You stared him down in a pool
of greatness he'd drown in, a slow drunken
gasping for air but surfacing again and again –
and you? You had nothing to prove:
just livin' and livin' quick –
and, oh brother – smack – right
between the eyes, the killer-diller
in your clubbing hands, the undertaker's silence

in your eyes – you were Mister *Night Train*,
Mister "Put-'em-To-Sleep-With-One-Big-Hit."
And we're waiting for you
to come from the grave, Sonny,
to tell us how to see the past
because we got one sad man
still hanging on here:

every now and then he comes up for air:
we hear him on the waves, his face a worn out speed bag,
the skin puffy, the bloated smile looming
for that last big crack: a balloon waiting for
the end needle: pop-pop –
he's a black Elvis ready to fall.
Women sue him for child support –

his brain's all lost – and it's all
that sea of troubles that Archie knew
he'd own: you see, Sonny, he's deferred
a lot of hurt and you have to laugh
because it all-honest-to-God
comes down to smack, smack, bang
in the blood –

                    like you:

the goon for hire, a six-foot, one-inch,
two-hundred and eighteen pound
bull-shouldered mugger whose thick fists
never held the right words and your wife, Geraldine,
lying about your undressing for bed,
that last fall backward, a king-size toppling over,
drugged, listless – dead on dead.

In the dark undercurrents of rumor
that wash over all the statistics,
the facts of how you left your twenty-five
brothers and sisters to become
your nineteen arrests by age eighteen,
all your ties to the big bad white guys –
"Peppy" Barone, Frankie Carbo, Johnny Vitale,

"Blinky" Palermo – two stories alone survive:
how the unnamed rich white cat
took his mistress, your kin, maimed her
and called your hand into murder –
how the price of scandal
was a trumped-up assault charge
that sent you to the jail rooms of extortion:

In the dark harbored quiet of prison nights,
Muslim words flashing like polished blades
in the alley's moonlight, seven men
sell you on how to play the hand
of the devious oaf going down
for a new black Moses who will rise up
in the promise of a new chanting –

and you listen in the silence of memory:
Birmingham, the four girls, and those white
press boys carving up your words
I'm ashamed to be called an American
into the bad man language
of the only story we need:
the good, the bad.

The time is now, Sonny,
for we're gathered here to keep the question:
Was it heroin or "Blinky's" boys that used you up?
Did Malcolm's prophets press-gang your brain?
Did you lose or did you dive?
We need it clean. Clay has been betrayed,
made the dope, and, if you could come back, Sonny,
you'd weep to see yourself
in him. You'd go on a series of knockouts
that'd leave us all reeling
or go back on the street, money in hand,
laughing all the way
to the next grave because all fighters
go down on their backs –

all fathers die into some memory –
and you, childless, an instrument of myth,
son of a father who lost the count,
can come forth to stand before all boxers
who now stand after your past,
you, the Cain and the Judas, you, the bad guy,
the marked man, the brutal bear who gave Cassius his name.

Prescient

The night before he KO'd Jimmy Doyle,
he saw the death in dream, in hands, open,
his own, fingers closing, and fists –
an eighth round killing that he swore he saw,
the story he told to commissioners
who would not hear him, a premonition
reporters refused to believe,
he, Walker Smith, the sweet one,
the greatest pound for pound in the history
of anything and everything that counts,
saw Doyle on the canvas, face down, bloody,
the referee moving in for the count,
saw the bulbs popping, the jabbing of light,
saw Turpin and Zale, Olson and Fulmer,
Graziano and Maxim, LaMotta
and Basilio – the crosses and hooks,
his brain going down, a quitting
that comes from knowing how things end
the night before the first bell rings –
206 fights, 109 KOs, thirty years of boxing,
and one man dead.

Middleweight

for Martin Espada

You learned early on the anger of want.
Schooled in slum's hatred, your fists
began the beating of the heavy bag
to the dream of Hagler and Monzon,
The Marvelous One, *The Shotgun*,
boxers whose canvas you envied.

You never studied. Late for class,
behind in words, you sat in your corner
and stared me down. Undefeated
with eight straight knockouts,
you ducked every instruction I gave.
Your eyes skipped rope until the bell
ended each class and tallied our points.

Like *Escopeta*, Argentina's James Dean,
you were our city's new bad boy,
 a young star whose troubled nights
brought sirens and the cruiser's blue light.
When I called you out for copied work,
you squared off in a stance that you called
"the hands of stone." In the gloveless
language of knuckles, you held them up in front of me
to talk the parties and the girls of your world.

When your stablemate took you out
in a Saturday night defeat,
I attended to the lessons of my life.
Your funeral mass, a field of black orchids
and weeping teenagers, didn't even make
the front page of *The Brockton Enterprise*.

Sometimes, late at night, watching the fighters
jab and feint across the screen,
I think of how it might have gone the other way:
you're walking Italian streets with a starlet

on each arm, smiling, your muscled torso
still ready for anything that comes your way.
It was fifty-fifty at best, and you, a longshot,
went down with a hole in your back.

Home Movies

for #10, the star

Like those first newsreels, we all move too fast,
solid foot soldiers who block out the sound
and fade in the dark and grainy fame film.
And then number ten, the quick one, breaks loose:
always in the lead, he outruns the film
into the shadows – the band plays unheard
and the cheerleaders flash once, their faces
buried beneath dead cheers that float up
through the crowd's silent wave of arms
into that spliced and gray day we fingered
the falling sun, our arms flexed in surf.

We scream and stagger, naked warriors
who whoop at the waves that take us under
into the savage dark of undertow,
deep in the drunk cold of each pounding wave
and held by the drum beating sound of sea
which rolls us over until we surface
in a circle and cry out the last cheer,
bobbing in the coming twilight, yelling
for the star to come up and break open –
slip free from our dumb screams and break away
from the ocean's mute, dark, and deadly roar.

A.I.D.S.

Up that three story tenement climb,
she knocks, enters, and finds
"G. G." lined in gold chains,
his braids all undone,
his mind singing along
with island songs.

The blinds are roped
down. The rug smells like feces,
and his legs, incrusted
in the urine of a week,
won't move. Lean
as a prophet, he yields,
but when she tries to stick him,
he screams, "Oh no, lady, lady – no, no –
not that vein. This one. Only this one only
or I will kill you." She gives in
and goes with the vein
he swears by. She sets him up,
leaves him with meds and instructions
he will not hear. He just keeps singing,
a tape about to click off.

At home she showers
and showers and comes out
reeling. Her family has had enough
and they want her out. She says
she won't go back
to "G. G." and his I. V.
or the thirteen year old girl
just up from Haiti, pregnant, her eyes
two black dimes of death.

But she does. Each Sunday
she's pulled out of swimming
pools into rooms of junk.
She drives back in
to mount the stairs

and do it again: she helps
"G. G.'s" arm under the lamp,
and, pushing the needle in,
measures each pulse,
each beat counted and held,
each breath almost more
than money can buy.

What the Nun Told Me

changed the flight of geese
rising from the pond where the boy,
Steven Bordonaro, drowned. It changed

the way my wife smiles and the longing
we bring to the wakes of children.
It eliminated salvation, forgot the entropy

of the sun, the freezing land. She told me
how to walk around the hospital, to look
inside, to believe in circles, the crocus,

the light off a Datsun's chrome,
bluejays scattering wrens – why, that's
the way, she said. She said pray

for the black elk you've never seen,
bow into victims you would never
have held, study the faces we all

would have stoned. Understand how
the marsh constricts. Memorize how
the river moves. Remember Latin,

the grammar of row upon row of stacked
flesh. She said learn it all. Study hard.
Pray for that boy and do it now.

Alchemist

An old man plods the hill,
turns into a man I know.
He steps into the gray
light of the March morning.
He cries like my mother
when she was young, weeping
rosaries in her room.
He limps, is a killer
who wears a mask to keep alive:
Today, a soldier after war
whose chameleon eyes flicker blue and black
and turn steel gray. His skin is ash.

My oldest daughter calls
from the next room: She cries
over homework and the man's cat-call
breaks into our house.
He holds coins that change into
discs that cover the eyes
of dead men. He becomes that man
loading trash barrels into the back
of the Chevy wagon on Saturday mornings,
who says, "There is never only one way."
I hear that voice as kind
as the autumn mornings he tried
to change me into him.
But it's fool's voice: It turns iron
and my daughter is still.

He trudges closer. I run to him
but he does not know me. She yells
from the porch steps, whipping her arm
up and around, calling us home.
His face is stone, and she screams
in fear of magic, knowing
I can change him – he can change me –
it is all in the mix of the image –
an April morning, the light just right,

the wind opening the maples' sap,
the new leaves of old words
hung in the air like small corpses
waiting to be buried, forgotten
in the magician's green that covers everything.
But I move fast –
he has found the speed of a dying man.

He grows thin, sneers, ages like
a good idea that gets away,
and takes the pace of a mad man.
I run as if in miracle, trying to reach
him before he turns back to stone,
to dust, to make him say,
child, child – my own
running coming to a twenty year end
of pushing for air, the urge
to convert the absence of light
into color, a face,

this face that I see now,
that is always a part of me,
escaping and disappearing,
coming to life in faceless dreams
that scar to the surface
of a story that she tries to pull me
out of – now, running at the heart of magic –
shouting, crying
that there is nothing there
but air.

Wild Hart

It has crossed over again,
come out too far, and is ready:
in the quickest of starts
it will be running in the memory
of old wounds, the opening of the heart.

A generation gone, December flight
through brambles, antlers closhing into branches,
it knows the jacklighter's fierce, bright eye.
It remembers escape, backtracking
in November wind, the pulse for flight,
the long life of caution from risk
of going down in the bleeding October sun.
Survivor of the staggering in of winter
and its buckshot, its killing white,
it dreams snow as high as a fawn,
a frozen hind caught in the deep,
the hunger for lichen and moss.

Today, its muscles tense, shudder
in desire for sudden motion:
In this late October morning of chance,
it comes from the tree line
into the sage, that clean-sighted
world of danger, its heart beating in risk.
And love,

quivering, trying to shake off the buck
fever, I freeze on the trigger.

The Deadman's Hand

If you had your way, the script would have been
as grand as Caesar, Wild Bill and Brutus,
Jack McCall's bullet, the back of your head,
the legend written for generations –
still, those four black cards, the aces and eights,

and the diamond jack, remind us to keep
our backs to the wall. At Nuttal & Mann's
Number 10 saloon, you broke your own rule:
careless stuff, Hickok – the gunfighter knows
the world is on him, the odds in favor

of the drunk drifter in search of a name.
Was it the whiskey? Your wife, so distant
that you longed for love? You should have cashed in,
returned to your room, polished your ivory
handles, and fallen asleep to the dreams

of prairie flowers, the earth stilled with thick,
black loam – or an exotic butterfly
as quick as your draw, your hand reaching for
your pistol, your life, Troy Grove to Rock Creek,
Custer to Cody, from Abilene to

Deadwood Gulch, your hand playing toward this
last fight, Kiowa and Arapaho
standing on a distant hillock, waiting
for the gold-haired scout to draw, to fire,
to kill – oh, Wild Bill, it's lodged in your brain.

Gymnastics

for Sister Rose Immaculata

Floor, beam, and vault
champion,
coming Tuesday afternoons
for extra help
to improve her mathematics,
she turns his life
upside down
in a tumble
that numbers
will not solve –
he can count the digits
on a hand: the years between
them an equation
he will not
violate.

She dons
the school colors,
purple and white,
like a saint
parading before nuns.
Courted by gold medals,
she wins every meet.
Still, the figures
haunt her, the answers
never correct.
Held in his own iron cross,
he studies the violet girl
with her geometric shape:
she hunches above
formulas
he knows by heart.

Little thing
to give her a B:
he, too, cannot remember –

has forgotten the young woman
in her habit,
the one who made him
memorize her Latin,
the conjugations
that have flipped
out of his mind.

Love Poems in June

1.

My daughter stands lost
in the chorus. Her debut
is frightening. It is *Monster Madness*,
a school girl's play, and her shyness
scares her back behind a tombstone prop
where she dares the impossible:
real terror.

"This is a grave situation,"
says a child Dracula,
and I fear for her
practiced lines, her eyes
hypnotized in lights,
these moments when I cannot
hold her—she is moving,
saying something about werewolves
and then, of course, she has forgotten,
the silence ghostly, looming up
between us.
Her lips struggle to scream
the lines of horrible wonder,
the words in the heart of quiet,
that place where love makes its secrets
and keeps them safe from everyone.

2.

Behind their texts,
they are in love with love,
daydreaming all the songs,
albums full of heaven,
bearded rock stars and thin girls
with sharp bones who sing it out
on the radio: love.
They study Donne
and have answers I have forgotten.

They tell me love is kind
of like a dream you make

come true. I'd tell them
it is a poem you never write,
or, once written, put in a book
to lie in form. If pressed,
I'd say it has no shape:
it is something close to
a desire for protection.
It is all they want to know,
all that matters: love.
Their stories are lined with it.
Their poems are jammed
with its song of kindness.

3.

The rain is an old song
I keep trying to learn.
It is hard. There are moments
when the sound is close to love
and it confuses me.
The dead sing in this rain:
I have heard them
in the wind, forgiving
the living for all our lies of love.
Love: I say it again and again
until it breaks like rain,
until it freezes on my lips.

Desire

We cup our hands to hold what we want
and then it's gone. Like water
or the first time you lie to your sister.
When the score is tied, you drop
that touchdown pass. Your sister needs
to know if Bobby, the shortest love of her life,
is cheating.
In the biggest game
of a year we never forget,
you run that hook and go
and you're going long, the high
arcing spiral beginning to fall,
and you feel that perfect lead,
the glory of being alone under lights
that cheer – that leap that takes you
into the air, a dive from a cliff
in a dream you always forget,
the ball brushing the tips of your fingers –
and your sister finding you
out – how you and Bobby
drove two girls to the mountains
for the weekend, for love. She says,
"It's okay. Forget it."
And you want it. You've got it.
The ball feels your hands
and you can touch love.
Safety and a grace of sorts –
you had it once.

ELEGIES

The Crushed Stone Death of William Smith:
Bird and Son, Walpole, MA, 1982

In April, we found bits that weren't cleaned out,
feathery flesh stuck to the pit's walls.
Navinsky said it looked like "glitter,"
the mica-like flecks of the splintered bones.

Timber loose, the dock's rotting skirt gave way
and Smith fell into the grinding machine:
his skull and skin butterflied into blood
that sprayed the granite slabs and jeweled the bin.

In the knotted second before our screams,
our held chests sickled. Our torsos anchored,
we were no more than museum pieces
until *shit it down* cranked us back to life.

In May, I quit rock, cut ten penny nails
and thousands of asphalt roofing shingles.
I tendered the machines and oiled their parts
as if they were bodies of accident.

Billy Smith, a kid two weeks on the job,
turned us toward anger, his life cremated
into the gear-grinding sound that owned us:
we became spare parts, sad words and bad blood.

That July, I rose from the dinner table,
Sunday afternoon, weeping Smith's death
in story pieces that moved my son's wife
into wide-eyed grief - - I couldn't finish.

Monday night, finishing my graveyard shift,
I returned to the dock to weep again.
I held the new safety railing. I hummed
a hymn whose words I could not remember.

I knelt down and fanned my hands on the dock's

new planks shellacked in the moon's gulled light.
I went back inside to my old machine
and, like a savage, all night long, cut stone.

Burial, Late February

Sparrows and squirrels, a birch lit
by early morning sun: the snowdrop dogwood,
forsythia, the scent of lilacs and roses –
what the mind can hold,
cliché's brute-nosed truth, squalid,
muddied, that digging down, inexorably
into the heart:
the murmur of a glacier beginning
to crack –

                                        leaves

at the clearing's edge, wind gusts in the vineyard,
pans rattling in a kitchen, a cigarette lit,
children at the fireside –

                                        and rain

on the windowpane, like weeping,
like glasses clinking at betrothal –

                                        that iceblink

that blinds the eye,
like freezing, like phlegm congealing,
like everything that the world calls cold.

Death Squad

When the nuns lined up
in that gully that stretched out
like a long birth canal,
they prayed to Jesus
in their make-shift prayer –
the crashed engine steamed
in the Salvadoran heat
as they caught the sound
of the popping M-16s
and waited for the breathless
beating of their angels' wings.

Slots

I knew her,
the woman who walked out
of the casino and drowned herself
in the tribal pond.
In the early March dusk,
she gave up her last syllables
to a mute scrawl of the back
of an ATM receipt:
she was sorry that money
was more than breathing
into the next morning.
Cars collect at her house.
A neighbor says her husband
is under sedation. His parents
are caring for the children.
He should have seen it coming –
her left cheek twitching,
her eyes – that look:
you can tell when someone is in trouble.
It's like the sound of birds wheeling
in the sky before a blizzard.
Most people don't notice.
They get into their cars and drive
to the quotidian pulse that beats them
from one day to the next.
Then it comes – the inexorable white
that fills the town for three days,
the streets defeating the plow trucks,
the schools shut down,
the neighborhood rallying to dig out
as the sky lightens and the wind disappears.
The storm forgotten, we return
to what we must do,
cautious, though, of the ice,
the ruts in the road – and feeling
that ache in the muscles,
the wake of shoveling
that stays for the few days

it takes for it to all melt,
to pool and trickle away,
the landscape in its promise
to come back a lush green.

The Weatherwoman

predicted the speed of collapse.
Hurricane after hurricane, we tuned in
to watch the floods, the cadavers
washed up on city streets.
That summer she reported
the facts and numbers
like a ballerina bowing before applause.
Each night she appeared
in a new skirt and an angelic smile.

My wife and I loved her.
We took note of every change:
her haircut, those hurried words,
her loss of weight.
One night a dark-haired man
replaced her.
His voice reminded us
of an old friend,
and then, after a week without her voice,
she was back, cherry and bright
as the hope in a change of season.
An umbrella on her shoulder,
she forecast the sun and a long, dry spell.
That evening she was brilliant.
She thanked her viewers for their cards
and told us that "love takes us
to the strangest of places."

We never saw her again,
this woman of sky and clouds and rain.
She was the girl who had the world,
who had the day's weather to report,
the one who never returned,
our girl, the girl we always had to watch.

Hard Heart

The boy explains his poem,
the Saco River overflowing its bones.

In the cities of our country
sisters are lost:

      sleeping:

listen to the tick
of oxygen in Taiwan bars,
hear the leaves in the beams of light,
a car swishing along an unlit road.

      Essays.
      Letters of recommendation.

(abducted? stolen?)

Why does the radical mind grow old?
Repetition is the handmaiden of failure.
Repetition = victory.

(conservative?)
(hold?)

It is the river, always the river:
coursing
in search of the fifth season.

x=x=x
The question is the question of number.
Relative? Relatives?

Quit playing around:
today the snow is falling
on the campus grounds.

Students, muffled, pass by.
Winter is coming:
ice: cold: old:

come home, little girl,
come home.

The Young Girl Who Came with Poems

You were silent, a blonde hope
with eyes like a saint.
You always came to class alone
and brought thin books of poetry.
I still keep your paintings, your gifts:
a Madonna veiled in flames;
grackles and martins attacking
a marauding crow like small, dark angels.
In a folder, I save your notes,
poems, letters I could never answer.

You came with persistent laughter,
congested lungs, wheezing stories of love,
and endless poems that kept rolling
from your pocketbook like marbles.
You wanted more than praise, more than
any criticism could give.

Today, with December as hard
as it should be, I thought of you.
In my backyard a wren lay frozen
on a bed of dry leaves.
I cupped it in my hands with the frozen dirt
and hesitated, then hurled it
at the ice-lined, barbed wire fence,
pretending it shook its wings and was gone.

Mount Hood

Waking to the tick
and beep
of machines

                 he cannot see:
eyes blinking,
taking on fluorescent light
in the twitch of his body,

a cadaver
entering the world of breath,

tube in his mouth, his fingers touching it:
the boys back
               in his brain:
chopper circling above him,
Larson, Navickus, Walsh and Stone,
shouting,
               huddling over the bodies
with him,
hoisting them out of the snow,
their faces blue and puffy,

lips stitched
           with ice.

The ropes, the copter's blades:
the giant bug whirring into the sky
and then the rolling down the mountain,

Stone rubbing his hands, saying
"We got them," telling the story
of his ancestors, the homesteaders,
The Children's Blizzard, forty degrees

           below zero,

hundreds dead on the drifted prairie,

dozens of boys and girls caught
in place,
upright,

walking home from school,
manikins frozen
                    into statues by a monster
no one foretold – Stone holding on
to the words, his laughter turning ironic,

and, out of nowhere,
the storm coming back –
all of them dismissing
the train-like roar of wind, Larson

grabbing him,
white teeth flying across the sky –
its coming on,
                    crystals of ice sparking
their lips, a heavy-headed
howl exhausting its rumble –
and staying calm,
the staying, staying
until Larson's knees buckle

and he tumbles
down the slope, a rag doll swallowed
by the ravening white, the light
a bright darkness,
a touchless braille they enter,
crow-dark in its white blind –

panic that ordered the strength and speed
to get to Larson, to grip their ropes,
speak to each other in the pull

and tug
of direction – the crack of avalanche
reporting in the ravine.

That coming back, now,
to the storm's waning,
snow chalking a starless sky:
their torsos buried –
the palate beginning to freeze
and breath balling up in the lungs –
and dreaming: a room of flashbulbs
that don't stop popping,
a volley of needles that sting the skin,
and praying,

                    a rented breath that tries
to lift the body from the drift.

And the second waking,
a coming out
of the snow's silver,

his mind returning
to his lips and skin,
the ticking of the room,

the woman
                    he has loved,
his children and friends – he wants
his eyes to come out of the yellow and black
dots before him, to remember their names,
the boys he could not save,
their corpses

warm and dead.
And, so, his speech abiding the coma's letting go,
his patient tongue
waiting in rest,
numb,
almost bodiless,
floating,
a little thing,
silent, stunned, stung.

Broken Places

for Chuck Ozug

We collected around your coma, friends and family
congregating above a weak muscle of blood,
a piece of the heart broken off, crumbling
like a cake taken from the heat too soon.

In Vietnam, Glenn Menowski,
our childhood friend, stepped on a Claymore mine
that blew him apart. His squad found his flesh
in his helmet liner, on rocks and tree bark.
I remember how my mother and father broke up:
too much drink, cigarettes, young suicides
of the heart – all the bad spots congealing
like ice that builds on a tree's thin limb.

We know those places, can feel them the way
healed bones know the cold air of November.
What we recall, then, is a perfect dawn,
the hillside painted with December snow –

we climb that hill, the Christmas sled
cradled in our arms, the dream of descent
taking shape in a sky full of angels,
the whole world as clean as white tape.

Scouts

At Camp Squanto, we sat by the fire,
inductees arrow-marked by blood.
We held flint and steel and pledged Pawtuxet
allegiance to our new brothers in arms.

All his married life, the *Nisshoki* flag
hung in my father's closet. Red and white,
The Rising-Sun marked the Navy valor
he lost in women's bedrooms, the taverns

of squandered money, his funeral business
fingerprinted with padded bills, forged
invoices, the undercurrent of bad
blood, affairs gone wrong, and angry men.

Tisquantum made deals with Massasoit,
translated lies that brokered two lives.
Peacemaker, he died in poisoned fever,
blood trickling from his nostrils. My father's

blood, stroke-driven, collected in his ear
and dried in a knot on the lobe. I found
the box beneath the flag, Pacific love
letters from my mother and his mistress.

Old Squanto's face was on the treasured patch,
The Order of the Arrow, a secret
tribe for those who upheld the Oath and Law.
Surviving a night alone in the woods,

we became would-be soldiers, readying
for bamboo stakes and the Airborne Ranger
patch on our fatigues and dress blues. We were
boys, cocks of the walk, preparing

for history's thicket and the small boxes
of love to be hidden in the corners

of dark rooms, artifacts of lust
waiting to be found by the next in line.

Winter Song

You turn off the highway
and drive into the hills,
a gray light on the marsh
white with ice. You listen

to the engine shutting
down, step onto gravel
dusted in snow: one light
in the home, firewood

frozen in its neat stack,
a jay gliding between
the last hold of shadow
and a night, you remark,

coming with an east wind.
You feel the darkening,
the moon in its donning,
a distant, barking dog--

and the cold shivers us
toward blankets and sheets,
snow sifting from hemlocks,
this brimming, darkling night

ascending from the fields,
silent and still, the stars
beginning their sky dance,
the lake its cowled dream.

Comeback

Rocco Francis Marchegiano:
I met him once. He shook my hand,
said "Nice to meet you, kid," and looked
away, money on his mind.
I was with his nephew. I said
"Nice to meet you, champ," and looked
away. I was sixteen,
my own hits and licks on my mind.

Our city's legend retired
into a dull weight of fame—
overrated, underrated—
and death in 1969,
Newton, Iowa, a mangled plane.
His body flown home to Brockton,
to our family's funeral home,
my grandfather buried him—
my father, the embalmer, touched him up.
In 1970, I went to Des Moines, Iowa
to teach and met Lowell Coburn,
the young undertaker who shipped Rocky's corpse
back home to Brockton.
He lived next door. "Nice to meet you,"
he said. "Coincidence is what death can give us."

And when I returned to Brockton,
a beaten-up place with window grates
on Main Street's abandoned stores,
the steel defending against the nothing that is left,
I couldn't find the signs of my
old hometown. At George's Café,
one of the city's last landmarks,
I walked through its rooms to study
all the newspaper clippings and photos hanging
on the restaurant's walls.
I stalked each fight in search

of the city that was gone:
Below Rocky's photos, Ali snaps a left
through the bloody mouth of Cooper,
and Hagler's right cross clubs
the "Motor City Cobra's" chin,
a right, that night, as right as right,
the "Hit Man's" legs collapsing,
his eyes on queer street,
that bewildered look that takes me
back to the rings and heavy bags
of my youth, all the bad words,
the punches given and taken.

They come back to me like letters
through a chute, the forgotten words
of a boy who learned the lessons
that each fist delivered: fight
to the death, be willing to die
on each street corner,
every win and defeat another notch
in a reputation that tells you
who your are—

                              I was a dumb kid,
I say to myself, who has grown old and dumb,
neither embarrassed by it nor proud of it—
we were boys who grew up in our fists.

And, today, I wonder what Rocky would say
about *The Brockton Enterprise*'s front page news,
the heroin addiction infecting our city,
the headlines spreading across the country,
the White House announcing
the match between the government
and the bad batch of stuff
that's killing our city's immigrants
in staggering numbers, the newspapers recording

each day's deaths like judges scoring the rounds
of a one-sided fight.

                  And I remember my grandfather
chalking the names of the deceased on his blackboard,
the posting of the wakes and funerals.

I stare Rocky down once more.
Hanging high above the other boxers,
his right arm is raised in victory,
and that right hand, famous,
now, and then, is always
coming back to me, heroic
in that night of near defeat against Walcott,
our champ coming back in the thirteenth round,
that right smashing into Jersey Joe's jaw,
a bullet in a bolt that locks shut--
what we had and can never get back.

Shaving

In front of the sink's mirror, straightedge at your cheek,
the stainless steel glistening under fluorescent light,
you showed me how not to draw the blood, instruction,
in a quick-time cadence, that held for a lifetime of cleaning up to face the day.
USN mug in hand, the soap's lather dribbling
on the blue logo emblazoned on porcelain,
you talked V-J Day and "Bull" Halsey, FDR and Churchill on your tongue
in treasured words that gave you what she couldn't--what all the women
of a short life's fouling
could not.

               You sailed into the corners of our city to find glory,
hero-thirsty for honor, a fiction you had to have as truth. Tall enough to stand
beside you, I grew into your embalming. Hovering over Mrs. O'Brien's cadaver
you held your trochar like the magician's wand.
               You showed me how to drain blood
from the body's cavity, explained the push and pull of the trochar,
and we cut Margaret O'Brien
like would-be surgeons: the undertaker and his son.
I stood

                                 boy strong,
apprentice-to-man ready to take in each word—
shaving   again   listening

                               not knowing
I would soon don my own uniform

                               olive drab
second lieutenant's bars

                    to watch a war secondhand—

my classmates cut down in rice paddies
while I sat at a desk and counted bodies—
all the corpses we buried

                      whiskey and wakes

                              homburgs

and black suits
white shirts and black ties,
funeral masses and graveside eulogies—

standing like sentinels in the priests' words of death and resurrection.

Dead old man who died too young,
who squandered his life in barrooms and bedrooms,
who left his life on the deck of the USS Yorktown,
we have to come to our end:
I am through with all the poems that I have written on page after page
in magazines that become nothing more than resume´ publications.
I have written the words of the dead too many times.
You and I are done:
                      you, whom I still love beyond
all truth, and your aging son, who no longer owns the straightedge,
whose own dream of honor has been drained out of his body,
bled out like all the corpses you washed and dressed,
their hair combed, their cheeks rouged, their lips set straight,
each one shaved, a manikin ready to face the living.

Fomite

A fomite is a medium capable of transmitting infectious organisms from one individual to another.

"The activity of art is based on the capacity of people to be infected by the feelings of others." Tolstoy, *What Is Art?*

Writing a review on Amazon, Good Reads, Shelfari, Library Thing or other social media sites for readers will help the progress of independent publishing. To submit a review, go to the book page on any of the sites and follow the links for reviews. Books from independent presses rely on reader to reader communications.

Visit http://www.fomitepress.com/FOMITE/Our_Books.html for more information or to order any of our books.

As It Is On Earth
Peter M Wheelwright

Dons of Time
Greg Guma

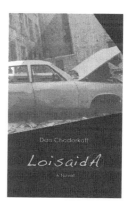

Loisaida
Dan Chodorkoff

My Father's Keeper
Andrew Potok

My God, What Have We Done
Susan V Weiss

Rafi's World
Fred Russell

Fomite

The Co-Conspirator's Tale
Ron Jacobs

Short Order Frame Up
Ron Jacobs

All the Sinners Saints
Ron Jacobs

Travers' Inferno
L. E. Smith

The Consequence of Gesture
L. E. Smith

Raven or Crow
Joshua Amses

Sinfonia Bulgarica
Zdravka Evtimova

The Good Muslim
of Jackson Heights
Jaysinh Birjépatil

The Moment Before an Injury
Joshua Amses

Fomite

The Return of
Jason Green
Suzi Wizowaty

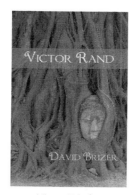

Victor Rand
David Brizeri

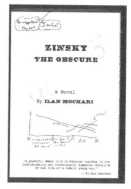

Zinsky the Obscure
Ilan Mochari

Body of Work
Andrei Guruianu

Carts and Other Stories
Zdravka Evtimova

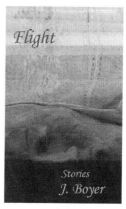

Flight
Jay Boyer

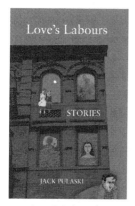

Love's Labours
Jack Pulaski

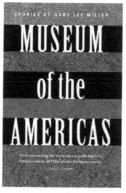

Museum of the Americas
Gary Lee Miller

Saturday Night at Magellan's
Charles Rafferty

Fomite

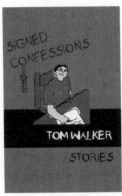

Signed Confessions
Tom Walker

Still Time
Michael Cocchiarale

Suite for Three Voices
Derek Furr

Unfinished Stories of Girls
Catherine Zobal Dent

Views Cost Extra
L. E. Smith

Visiting Hours
Jennifer Anne Moses

When You Remeber
Deir Yassin
R. L. Green

Alfabestiaro
Antonello Borra

Cycling in Plato's Cave
David Cavanagh

Fomite

AlphaBetaBestiario
Antonello Borra

Entanglements
Tony Magistrale

Everyone Lives Here
Sharon Webster

Four-Way Stop
Sherry Olson

Improvisational
Arguments
Anna Faktorovitch

Loosestrife
Greg Delanty

Meanwell
Janice Miller Potter

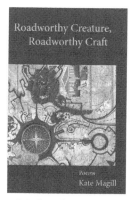

Roadworthy Creature
Roadworth Craft
Kate Magill

The Derivation of
Cowboys & Indians
Joseph D. Reich

Fomite

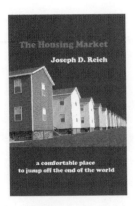

The Housing Market
Joseph D. Reich

The Empty Notebook
Interrogates Itself
Susan Thomas

The Hundred Yard
Dash Man
Barry Goldensohn

The Listener Aspires
to the Condition of Music
Barry Goldensohn

The Way None
of This Happened
Mike Breiner

Screwed
Stephen Goldberg

Planet Kasper
Peter Schumann

33929404R00065

Made in the USA
Charleston, SC
27 September 2014